Avoid being a 1920's Gangster!

Written by
Rupert Matthews

Illustrated by
Mark Bergin

Created and designed by
David Salariya

The Danger Zone

Contents

Introduction

The city of Chicago in the 1920s is an exciting place to live. Some people have become very rich in the business boom – unfortunately you and your brother Tony haven't! You need to figure out how to make a living in this busy city.

In 1920, the American government made it illegal to own or sell alcoholic drinks, a law called 'Prohibition'. In Chicago, organised crime has flourished as gangs of criminals make or import alcohol to be sold throughout the USA. But you don't want to make money illegally!

Police try to find and destroy the alcohol, often by pouring drinks down the drain.

This is you.   *This is your brother, Tony.*

On the streets

You've just graduated and Tony recently lost his job. So the first thing you need to do is get work. If you don't have any work, you won't get paid – and without money, you might starve. There are lots of jobs on offer in Chicago, but many youngsters are looking for work – not just you and Tony. You end up walking miles every day just trying to find somewhere that is offering a job. Even if you do find a vacancy, somebody else might get the job instead of you. You and your brother Tony are quickly running out of money – you're getting desperate.

THE MOVIE STUDIOS in the town of Hollywood provide work for lots of people. But first you need the money to get there. Can't afford the train fare? Tough! The inspector won't let you travel.

SOME PEOPLE find work on farms, but you grew up in the city – you don't have a clue about farming. Besides, there aren't many fields in Chicago.

FACTORIES often need workers. But they only hire skilled people who are recommended by existing staff. If you don't know any workers, you're out of luck.

YOU COULD WORK in a shop, but most are family businesses. You'll only get a job if a relative owns the store. Born into the wrong family? Forget it.

Into the gang

Tony suggests that you both join the police. The Chicago police need people who are tough, honest and know the area. Even better, you don't need lots of experience – they'll train you once you've got the job. They will even give you a smart new uniform, so you don't need to buy new clothes.

Tony gets a job patrolling the streets of Chicago, while you volunteer to work undercover. You're going to pretend to be a Chicago gangster! But it's dangerous work. If the gangsters learn that you're working for the police, you'll be in big trouble.

YOU START your undercover career as a street sweeper. That way you can pay attention to what the gangsters do, but no-one will think to pay attention to you.

Don't ask any questions, got that?

THANKS TO HIS smart clothes and fancy car, the local gangster should be easy to spot. Treat him with respect – hold his car door open for him.

THE GANGSTER decides that he likes you, so he asks you to do him a favour – deliver a package to an address. But he doesn't pay you – at least, not at first.

YOU KEEP your brother Tony informed about what the gangsters are doing. You show him the package that you have to deliver so that he can record it as evidence.

Numbers racket

The gangsters give you your first job – you'll be running an illegal gambling operation on the streets. This 'numbers racket' involves only small amounts of money, so it's a good way for the gang to find out if you can be trusted – without risking too much cash. Most of the bets you take are on horse races. You need to be able to do quick sums so that you can keep up to date with the betting odds, who has bet how much and what they have won – or lost.

GAMBLING is illegal and only Tony knows you are undercover. Any other police office will try to arrest you.

ALL GAMBLING is done in cash. Your job is to make money, so don't offer generous odds to the gamblers. You hand over the profits to the gang immediately. If you lose money, you'll be in trouble.

YOU KEEP careful records of bets that are made. Punters want their money fast if they win a bet. If you keep them waiting for their money, they might turn nasty!

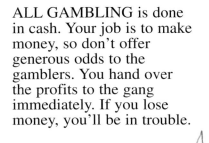

EACH GANG has its own 'territory', or area of Chicago. Only members of that gang are allowed to take bets in that area. Always stick to your own gang's territory – if you walk around the wrong corner you'll find yourself in serious trouble with another gang.

ONCE A PERSON has made a bet on a race, you give them a receipt stating how much they have bet. The receipt also states what horse they have bet on and how much money they will get if their horse wins the race.

The gambling den

Richer gamblers play cards, roulette and dice games at special gambling dens. These clubs are open only to people who have been invited by gangsters. You've proved yourself to the gang, so they decide you're to work in a gambling den. You must dress smartly, be polite to the gamblers and learn lots of new ways to part people from their money.

The games are arranged so that gamblers don't win very often. Most of the money is kept by the gambling den and passed on to the gang. People known to be gangsters don't work at the den – if they did, gamblers would be less likely to spend money.

I've never seen so much money!

If people only knew...

SLOT MACHINES are meant to pay out a set proportion of the money they take. Your job is to rig the machines so that they pay out less money.

THE ROULETTE WHEEL needs an quick-witted person to keep an eye on the ball. An experienced gang member teaches you how to run it.

POKER calls for skilful card control. You deal the cards, making sure nobody cheats by slipping a spare card out of their sleeve.

Handy hint

Never gamble yourself. All the games are rigged so that the gang wins as much money as possible.

Better luck next time.

YOU WORK as a cashier only after learning all the other jobs. The gang trusts very few people to handle so much money.

AT THE END of the day you carry the den's takings to the gang headquarters. Watch out for rival gangsters who might try to mug you for the cash.

YOU REGULARLY keep in touch with Tony. Your records tell him how much money is being gambled, and who is doing the gambling.

Spying in the speakeasy

Odd jobs

ONLY PEOPLE trusted by the gang are let into the speakeasy. As doorkeeper, you have a list of these people. Let the wrong person in and you'll be in trouble.

ost of the gang's money comes from selling illegal drinks. Beer and whisky are cheap to make, but people will pay high prices for them, especially if they are sold in a 'speakeasy'. Speakeasies are clubs where entertainers perform while people relax, chat and drink.

Tony tells you the police are planning a raid on your gang's speakeasy. You let him know when the most customers and gangsters will be there, so that the police can arrest as many people as possible. But be careful not to blow your cover!

AS COMPERE, you introduce the glamorous singers and stage acts. You might even get to meet a Hollywood movie star!

ANYONE WHO doesn't pay for their drinks or causes trouble is thrown out. Luckily only the tough gangsters do this work.

FIGHTS MIGHT break out late at night. Keep an eye open for trouble and dive for cover the moment anything kicks off.

THE ALCOHOLIC DRINKS served in the speakeasy are not what they seem. One of your jobs is to soak labels off the bottles of cheap drink and replace them with fake labels. This makes it seem as though the bottles contain expensive brands of drink.

Due north

I t is legal to make alcoholic drinks in Canada, so some gangsters buy booze there and smuggle it back to the USA. Because Canadian drinks are made legally, they are usually better quality than the illegal drinks made in the US – so they can be sold for higher prices. You are sent north to buy a load of beer and whisky to bring back to Chicago.

ALCOHOLIC DRINKS are allowed into the USA, but only for medical reasons or for scientific research. The gangsters get hold of an import licence, then make you change it so it looks as though you are allowed to import more booze.

IN CANADA you can relax and enjoy yourself. The gangsters can't watch what you are up to and you are not wanted by the police. Find a smart hotel and order yourself a great meal. Wonderful stuff!

YOU CAN USE the postal service without worrying that you are being watched. So you write out a complete account of everything that you have been doing recently and post it off to Tony.

ALL THE CASES of drink need to be counted and checked. You don't want any to be stolen.

The Royal Canadian Mounted Police (Mounties) can't stop you from taking drinks out of Canada – it's legal to export alcohol. But some Mounties warn the US authorities if they suspect you are smuggling drinks bound for America, so watch out!

The wheelman

Every gang needs a team of skilled drivers. These 'wheelmen' need to know how to keep cars in top condition, how to steal cars, but above all how to make a speedy getaway. You're being promoted fast and your gang is now using you as a wheelman. This means you can gather evidence as you meet important gang members and drive them around. And you will witness the gang's bank robberies, shoot-outs and other crimes.

THE BOSS does not want you listening to all his conversations. He tells you to stay out of earshot, but try to overhear as much as you can. Then you can pass the information on to Tony.

My arm is getting tired.

STAY ON your toes. You may be kept waiting for hours by the Boss, then have to spring into instant action.

THE BOSS likes his car to be clean and shiny all the time. You will spend hours washing and polishing.

STOLEN CARS are used during crimes. If you have to steal a car, watch out for its real owner.

MODERN CARS need lots of regular maintenance. You need to know basic mechanics or you could cause more problems than you solve.

Handy hint
Make sure you have enough petrol – you'll need it for your getaway.

I bet Tony doesn't have to put up with this!

BATTLES WITH rival gangs are terrifying. As the wheelman you have the job of getting fellow gangsters out of trouble – fast. Remember to duck out of the way of those bullets.

19

Running the protection racket

Sinister scare tactics

SMASHING shop windows is a frequent way of punishing shop owners who do not pay on time.

IF AN OWNER refuses to pay, the gang takes revenge by setting fire to their business, house or car.

MOST owners feel they have no choice but to pay the protection money. You are sent to collect it.

IF YOU WALK into the wrong territory, rival gangsters will try to grab the money you have collected. They won't ask nicely.

oon you are asked to help run a protection racket. This is a very profitable – and very unpleasant – way of making money. You are made to call on a business owner, bringing with you a pair of tough gangsters. Your gang offers to 'protect' the business against vandals and robbers. If the owner refuses to pay, the Boss sends gangsters to attack the business, causing expensive damage and sometimes injuring staff.

Each gang runs a protection racket in its own territory, but gangs often try to 'muscle in' on the territory of another gang. This can lead to gang warfare as one group of gangsters attacks another. Try to stay out of gang wars – they are extremely dangerous.

YOU KNOW which business the 'thugs' (tough gangsters) are going to attack. Tony has been promoted to detective, so you phone him up and tell him which businesses are being targeted. That way he can arrest the gangsters without you being involved.

21

Packing heat

I t's not long before you get to meet the Big Boss. He's big, tough and guarded by men who are 'packing heat', or carrying guns. These men are hardened criminals who have been in the gang for years – they are trusted by the Big Boss. They guard him from rival gangsters and are willing to use their guns at any moment. Be careful – you don't want to get on the wrong side of them.

CARRYING GUNS in public will only attract attention from the police. Most gangsters make sure guns are well hidden. A violin case makes a useful place to hide a tommy gun.

THE BIG BOSS is head of the entire gang. All the gangsters treat him with great respect.

BODYGUARDS are mean, rude and care only about the Big Boss. They push other people out of the way and won't listen to any complaints.

IF THERE IS a muddy puddle, the Big Boss will make you put your coat over it so that his expensive shoes stay clean.

Handy hint

Stay out of the way of the men packing heat. They are not likely to be nice to you.

AMMUNITION is bulky and heavy, but it must be kept where the gunmen can reach it easily. You'll find it in the most unexpected places!

Eh, Boss, I think I see the cops comin'.

YOU ARE SEARCHED by the gunmen now and then. They are looking for evidence that you are working for the police or for a rival gang.

He's clean.

He's lucky is what he is.

Money laundering

Money which has been stolen from banks can be identified by the police by the code numbers printed on the banknotes. The gangsters need to exchange this 'dirty' money for other money in a process known as money laundering.

The gangster who keeps the records of the financial transactions needs to be a clever mathematician and able to maintain accurate records in financial ledgers called 'the books'. You can't believe your luck when the gangsters make you a bookman – you will learn the gang's secrets. That means more evidence for the police!

THE GANG'S PROFITS are recorded in the books. That way, the Boss can make sure no-one is stealing his money. Rival gangs want to get their hands on this information, so keep the books safe.

GANGS RUN legal businesses in order to launder money. They get rid of dirty money by giving it to customers as change. Some gangsters also use dirty money to buy second-hand cars, then drive them round the corner and resell them for 'clean' money.

Here's your 'change', sir.

GANGSTERS ARE PAID in clean money, to distance them from the crimes they commit. Make sure that you don't muddle up dirty money and clean money.

THE BIG BOSS will keep an eye on the piles of cash that you handle as the bookman. He will expect you to keep all the books up to date.

You better be looking after my dough.

Handy hint

Don't let anyone get near the money. If it goes missing, the Boss will blame you.

YOU KEEP TWO identical sets of 'books'. One set is for the Big Boss, the other is for Tony.

The Boss

Y ou've impressed the Big Boss so much that he's going to make you the boss of a smaller gang. Each boss has his own territory to run on behalf of the Big Boss. You will organise all the gang's activities in your territory. You now have your own bodyguards, goons and a bookman. You may have to do some terrible things – stealing money from anyone you can, cheating at gambling and terrorising business owners. You will need to keep watch on your territory to ensure that no rival gangs try to muscle in to get 'a piece of the action'. But don't get carried away – you're still working undercover for the police!

Perks of the job

AS A GANG BOSS you can live in luxury – so long as you survive. Buy the very best food at the most expensive restaurants. Buy a fantastic house to live in.

HIRE STAFF to look after you in absolute comfort. You've earned it, right? Really you know your money is stolen from honest folk.

A SUDDEN BANG might be a door slamming shut, or it might be a gangster shooting at you. Living in fear is no fun, but that's life as a gangster.

Handy hint

Search all your visitors. They might be working for a rival gang.

Listen up, knuckleheads. I run this joint now.

RIVAL GANGS will try to have you murdered, or 'hit'. They could try to sneak up on you at any moment.

YOU MEET with other gang bosses to discuss criminal business and make deals. Make sure they don't trick you or the Big Boss will be very angry.

YOU ARE expected to wear expensive clothes. Go along to a tailor and get him to make you the very best suit he can, using only the finest cloth.

27

Final reckoning

YOUR EVIDENCE will be crucial. Use your records to explain how the gang made money from selling alcohol, gambling and threatening innocent people.

As soon as you have gathered enough evidence to convict the gangsters, you call in your brother Tony. He has the entire Chicago police force ready for a raid. You have taken huge risks to get information on the gangsters. Now it's payback time. You arrange for the police to arrive when the Big Boss and as many gangsters as possible are present, so that they can all be arrested.

Once the trial begins, you give evidence about the crimes that you have seen, how they were organised and which gangsters committed them. At last your double life as an undercover policeman is over. You have survived!

ONCE THE GANG has been jailed, the citizens of Chicago can live safely. Business owners no longer pay protection money and gunfire doesn't erupt in the street.

THE GANGSTERS go to prison. Prisons are tough places with small cells and harsh discipline. The Big Boss is sentenced to 'hard labour'. He has to do pointless tasks, such as smashing stones with a hammer.

AFTER THE TRIAL, everyone knows you were working for the police, so your undercover career is over. You join Tony as a detective and enjoy life.

Glossary

Betting odds A number to show what a gambler could win on a bet. If the betting odds are five-to-one, the gambler could win $5 for a $1 bet.

Bootlegger A person who smuggles illegal drinks. The word comes from the fact that some smugglers hid bottles of drink in their boots.

Cashier A person who handles cash. In a gambling club, they take money and give the players small plastic tokens called 'chips' with which to gamble.

Dirty money A slang term for stolen money.

Export To transport goods out of one place (usually a country) and into another.

Gangster A member of a criminal gang. Sometimes newspapers called any criminal a 'gangster' whether he or she was part of a gang or not.

Heat A slang term for a gun.

Hollywood A town in the US state of California. Many film studios are located there.

Import licence A government document that gives a person legal permission to import goods from one country to another.

Jazz A style of music. It originated in the southern US city of New Orleans, but during the 1920s it became popular across the USA.

Ledger A book in which financial records are kept.

Mountie A member of the Royal Canadian Mounted Police, which investigates serious crimes in Canada. At first Mounties rode horses, but nowadays most ride in cars.

Organised crime Crime that is carried out by large groups of criminals for the purpose of making money.

Poker A card game played by gamblers. Players seek to collect particular combinations of cards.

Prohibition The banning of alcoholic drinks such as beer, wine and whisky. In the USA alcoholic drinks were banned from 1920 until 1933.

Protection racket An illegal scheme that gangsters used to make money. Gangs would make business owners pay for 'protection' against thugs and thieves. If the business owner refused to pay, the gang would damage the shop and hurt the owner.

Punter A slang word for a gambler.

Racket A slang term for an illegal business scheme to make money.

Roulette A gambling game. A ball is flicked onto a spinning wheel marked with numbers. Players bet on which number the ball will land on.

Speakeasy A private club that sold illegal alcoholic drinks. The name comes from the fact that customers would be asked to speak 'easy' (quietly) when ordering a drink, in case there were undercover police in the club.

Territory The area in which a gang operates. Gangs often try to extend their territory at each other's expense.

Tommy gun A slang term for the machine gun made by the Thompson firearms company.

Undercover police Police who pretend to be somebody else – often a criminal – in order to gather evidence against criminals.

Index

A
alcohol 5, 14, 16, 17
ammunition 23

B
bear 17
beer 14, 16
Big Boss 22–23, 24, 25, 26, 27,
  28, 29
bodyguards 23
bookman 24, 25
books 24, 25
bootleggers 17
bullets 19

C
Canada 16, 17
cars 18, 19
Chicago 5, 6, 7, 16
clean money 24
clothes 23, 27

D
dirty money 24
disguise 21
drivers 18, 19

E
evidence 8, 18, 24, 28, 29

F
factories 6
farms 6

G
gambling 10–11, 12–13, 26
gambling den 12–13
gang territory 11, 20, 26
gang warfare 20
guns 22, 23, 26

H
Hollywood 6, 14

I
import licence 16

J
jazz music 7

L
local boss 8, 10, 18, 26

M
money laundering 24–25
Mounties 17

N
newspapers 11
numbers racket 10–11

P
poker 12
police 8, 9, 14, 26, 28, 29
prison 28, 29
Prohibition 5
protection racket 20–21, 28

R
robberies 18
roulette 12, 13
Royal Canadian Mounted Police
  17

S
slot machines 12
speakeasy 14–15

T
tommy gun 22
trial 28

V
violin case 22

W
wheelman 18–19
whisky 14, 16